Mirror Lake

David Van-Cauter

for Julia
(1970-2010)

ARENIG PRESS

First published in 2019
by Arenig Ltd (Arenig Press)
Dolfawr, Cwmrheidol, Aberystwyth SY23 3NB

Printed in UK by
4Edge Ltd, 22 Eldon Way, Hockley SS5 4AD

A CIP record for this book
is available from the British Library

ISBN : 978-1-9998491-3-9

Cover: Morning on Mirror Lake, Yosemite Valley
by Frederick Ferdinand Schafer (1839 - 1927)

IM Fell English font digitally reproduced by Igino Marini.
www.iginomarini.com

ACKNOWLEDGEMENTS

Some of these poems previously published by:
Ink, Sweat & Tears, The London Progressive Journal,
The Poetry Society, Ver Poets and Poetry ID.

Thanks to: Gareth Writer-Davies, Rachel Haynes,
John Mole, Helen Ivory, John Callaghan
and all members of Poetry ID, past and present,
for their help and support.

Mirror Lake

Piano

I hear you humming as you play
low at first
as if afraid to pin the melody
a timid voice through solemn strings
catching the notes
in an open envelope.

But soon the pace picks up -
your voice gains confidence
with each increasing scale.

Upstairs I close the door and try to concentrate.

The house is filling with your voice
now slightly out of key - it skips
and sticks to each imperfect beat:
a bird, caught by its claw.

That metronome, discarded, quivers
at the base, as keys are struck
more solidly, and the floorboards quake.

I scuttle down the stairs.
Suddenly you stop:
Sorry, was I disturbing you?
No, no, I say. *Keep playing.*

I walk into the kitchen
listen to you begin
that first, enquiring hum
that softer, timid touch.

A Flight

The air is overrated:
it's just a mix of gas, cloud, light -
nothing to write home about.

But when you power through it
at 30,000 feet
and it folds to your direction,

then you are held aloft,
so swift you feel motionless,
enraptured by its grip.

Elsewhere, grounded,
I think of your face, your hair,
your fear of heights.

This is our distance:
trails of gas, cloud, light -
nothing to keep us here.

Counting House

You were adding up the cost of things,
  calculating how,
by putting this much here, investing there,
  it would allow
more money to be saved, and less
  pissed up the tree,
more interest, less a compound of
  hard work and misery.

Money eats us from inside, it gnaws away
  at all that we possess.
The more we earn, the more we spend on items
  we don't need, and less
on bonds that bind our palms tight
  with a taut romantic glue.
You said that money matters -
  I disagreed with you,

and then the shouting started: I should pay more
  into our joint account,
how little you'd have left if you put in
  the same amount.
You'd worked it out exactly on the page,
  and when I said
your father was controlling your left hand,
  your mother, your head,

you laughed - although a simplified equation,
  it struck a nerve
somewhere within the black of our last statements,
  where our cash reserve
was draining from a fractured sense of self.
  Funny how a cheap smile brings
a change of heart,
  when adding up the cost of things.

A Walk

I left you on a bench and went exploring.
I thought I could get up the hill and back -
no complications -
but my feeble frame gave in:
the lungs, heavy with altitude,
burst suddenly, sent shockwaves to the throat,
the limbs so numb, they forgot their function.

By a crumbling wall I stopped, hunched over,
tried to look out at the wall of leaves
rising to a strip of sky.

I saw your father crossing fields from church to church
your green-tinged face on boating holidays
your mother telling you to concentrate
your sister walking off into the trees
your fragile line I cannot cross.

On my return, you said
How was the walk? Did it inspire you?
Well, I said, *it took my breath away*
not mentioning

the jagged contours
the sweep of yellow in the folds carved by the valley
the panoramic view

was you - it was all you.

Hoem

We scoured the Poets' estate - not the most
respectable of neighbourhoods, but one
where we could buy a place in Byron Close,
create our own inspiring *Hom Juan*,
and Keats Way felt romantic... When you said
to focus on the house and not the name,
I started looking at the walls instead:
these things enclose us all, and it's a shame
that houses can't be stanzas, with the streets
arranged in neat and metred patterns, poems
that stretch, interconnect, forming complete
collections and anthologies of homes.
You didn't like the area: too rough.
Poetic avenues aren't safe enough.

Bitter Lake

They came to build their dams,
irrigate the land,
make the soil rich and habitable.

But now the earth, infused with life,
was perfect breeding ground for poppies -
the people fed and loved them.

Seed pods slit by tiny knives
release a sap that's left to dry
and overnight, coagulates.

Stained brown, scraped and boiled,
then cured over hot flames,
it's sent back west,

where it infects
the offspring of the men
who came to build their dams.

I can see them still, like King Canute,
trying to hold back the tide,
armed with flowers of peace.

Admission

The house is dark without you.
I fumble towards the bathroom,
feel the piano lid,

the seat that's tucked beneath it,
tread down cold steps,

inch on tiptoe
past the low hum of the fridge,
the boiler's weary groan.

I could switch on the light,
admit defeat,
but the dark is comforting.

To break its blanket might wake you
miles away.

In the morning, eyes closed,
I'll bring you home.

Mong Khrum

In ancient Siam they would play a game, Mong Khrum,
involving dressing up, a gong, and giant drums;
two teams competed with each other to impress -
a world away from stately, intellectual chess
(although they played that too), and it's a tiresome thought
that many hundred years ago, the king and court
were just as entertained by show-offs, Gangnam-style,
as we remain today, their twirls and put-on smiles,
each craving for applause, then to be judged and marked.
Meanwhile, I sit and wonder in the vacant dark
which dance routine I'll choose myself tomorrow,
which of the multitude of tricks and bluffs I know
might work to get me through the day. The drums, the gong,
will play for me, and if I can, I'll play along.

Nothing We Can Do

Four words we dread:
they hover over us
like a cold wight.

The change is microscopic.
From the outside, only
paler skin, longer silences.

Our cat demands food,
bills must be paid,
packages retrieved, signed for.

We struggle to follow
TV narratives - tiny pixels
clashing on the surface.

Music cannot soothe us,
rage finds no voice,
life just trickles on.

The light is fading.
Nothing we can say,
nothing we can do.

Punakaiki, Paparoa

Out of the bus and into the rain - the first cloudburst for weeks
and the Punakaiki Pancake Rocks spread from the headland,
waiting to be drenched with thick Manuka honey:
line after line of limestone, sliced by surging waves
and blow-holes, orca whales breathing, showering the air.

I run ahead of the pack, looking for something I don't know,
snap photos, rows of tourists bypassed, gasping.
This is my escape, a cool climb into the overcast and cloudy chaos
of eroding rocks and clashing, crashing otherness -
no one can agree how these were formed, yet here they live,

always on the precipice of disappearance, every layer
vulnerable to the next explosive wave, or the next.
I cut a circuit, make my way to solid ground,
thinking of pancakes and honey and ocean spray,
carving curves into the coast, the distance.

Living Room

This is your space now -
sofas shifted to accommodate a hospital bed,
tables thick with medication,
drinks and flowers, get-well cards.

I am a visitor, bringing trays,
delivering takeaways,
fetching, carrying, helping you sit up.

We used to sit together,
my arms around you,
my fingers plaiting your hair
or pressing at your skin,
the cushions placed just so.

Today you pull your hair out
strand by strand, letting it collect
beside you on the bed,
each one a memory, unravelling,
a broken thought.

I watch you from a distance,
two metres feeling like light years.

Sometimes, when I touch your face,
a warmth connects us.
I feel it in your slight, barely perceptible smile,
imagine it behind your half-closed eyes.

And the living room lights up
with all we were, and are -
its long, slow breaths embracing us
in the space we have left.

Via

Saskatchewan in winter - open plains of wide
unknowable snow, stretching out like blank
unwritten pages, punctuated now and then by a tree
or a rock, or a trail of prints: not human soles
or tyre tracks, but some invisible creature
that calls this vast breath-freezing canvas home.

This journey's taken days, and from my cosy, snaking
viewing car, I try to capture snapshots, moments
as snowflakes, caught before they melt
inside this capsule, slowly meandering between
freight trains, expanding landscapes, tiny towns.

Blink and it's gone - this transitory place is guided by
old tracks and time that bends to a persistent rhythm:
gotta get up, gotta get out, gotta get there...
And somewhere in the space between departure and arrival,
I become one of my own photographs, a flaky outline
of a passenger, a blurring shadow, framed by frozen air.

Your Bloody Shoes

Your shoes were everywhere -
discarded in the random places where you sat,
kicked off after long days
teaching, marking, arguing -
Home and Away was your escape.
I'd cook for us.

I'd often trip and curse
your bloody shoes.
It was as if they'd sprung to life
and carefully positioned themselves,
aware of my approach, with two hot drinks,
a precarious tray.

I'd kick them grumpily away,
start that worn-down conversation
about getting a shoe rack.
You'd never use it anyway, I'd say.

.

That morning, as your strength was fading,
you said you couldn't feel your legs,
asked your mother to lift them, slowly,
one after the other, as if to march
defiantly, barefooted, to a place
where shoes are strewn on endless paths,
abandoned, scattered there
as dark ephemera.

Yours made their way to charity shops:
other walks, other homes.

Lost World

The earth's crust is so thin here
that the roads cave in, collapsing
into sinkholes, which they cordon off
or, in the roads, refill with gravel constantly
just to prevent the landscape and its people disappearing.

You would have hated this: a hundred-metre abseil,
and then a trek through rocks, insects and perilous drops,
the only exit a ladder climbing into darkness, chaos, light.

But you're not here, and so I fall and clamber
for both of us. I imagine your terrified face,
descending into the smoky, otherworldly air,
the rope and harness as the only barriers between
this place and the next, clinging for dear life.

We both make it down,
enjoy the glow worms glistening
like stars on the roof of the cave,
inventing constellations.

But the thirty-metre ladder is the hardest:
wet, muddy rungs and climbing hand by hand,
every ounce of strength in gradual dissipation,
the harness pulling, energising.

I wasn't brave today, but you - you put me to shame.
Hanging there, I caught a tiny glimpse of what you felt
staring into oblivion,
your lost world.

?

January in Canterbury
I remember library whispering
you answering
yes

Later we won the pub quiz
then pizza, fudge cake (my suggestion)
I didn't know you'd eaten
you too polite to say
I rambled on

We quizzed together two more times
before Valentine's Day
and that slushy rom-com, *JFK*,
three hours of questioning
confusion

You lied and said you liked it
I loved you for that

My card read
from ?
Yours, upside down
from J

Perspective

On another day
I could steer the boat
upstream, challenge the flow

and then, behind dark shades,
decide on my direction.

But those are different eyes
with unseen reflections
and the river is too slow.

I pass myself
halfway.

Reverse Space

The herbs have taken over now -
a path hidden beneath the arching spray
of mint and rosemary.

There is a pond beyond that hedge, behind
the empty bird feeder that swings
from the apple tree.

He used to push that lawnmower, the nonelectric
back-breaker, the green paint rusted
and all the blades blunt.

His wheelbarrow, with a hole the size of a skull,
provides a climbing frame for slugs,
storage for weeds.

His mind is elsewhere - his first love,
school uniforms and silent films,
songs from the music halls.

But as he sits, his eyes see through
each tendril hook, each patch of earth,
to the far, far end,

and buried there, the corrugated iron
of an Anderson shelter, still intact,
awaiting the next attack.

Long Shadows

A bright sunset this evening -
on the ground I am ten metres long,
an alien with wide-rimmed hat and carrier bags,
gliding through town from east to west,
in pursuit of my long shadow.

I ghost past restaurants, the market square,
the church, charity shops,
our meeting places, bolt-holes,
aiming for home,

but the sun is after me,
beating on my back like a shopping list:
reminders, reminders...

I climb our hill, as steep as ever,
my shadow a signpost,
longer and thinner now,

and for a second I see both of us
drifting up to the driveway,
laden with our heavy bags,

until we are delivered,
settled in another town
many miles from here,
our long shadows stretching further away
the more we let them lead us.

Mirror Lake

Ten years ago, Yosemite, in Spring,
we took the "easy" route to Mirror Lake,
you still fit enough to clamber over rocky paths for miles
until our lack of water finally defeated us
at the tiny bridge.

We ambled back another way, along a river
piled high with boulders as big as trucks.

It's Autumn now, and I retrace
as midges swarm around my face.
At every turn, I think I see you up ahead:
the path is winding differently.
Any moment now...

I find the bridge - it leads nowhere, poised like a painting,
and the sign for Mirror Lake points only to a dry plateau,
its water seasonal.

I stand within its circle,
breathe the panorama, such dry air.
You've gone, and now I can't recall
if we ever came here at all.

The ground reflects our footprints:
I try to follow them, but I'm blocked by rocks -
dead-end memories I've closed.
Were we here, or were we only passing through?

Mirror Lake consumes us in its folds,
as if I'm the one who died and you're alive,
walking backwards to seek out this place
ten years from now, remembering how
life suddenly dried up, absorbing us.

Snowgrip

The snow has come
my car wedged

its inches of icing
pockmarked with bird tracks

In blanket and dressing gown
I watch others graft

with shovels
enabling my escape

They scrape away cold scraps
hack at raw earth

I feel friction in the window pane
and through the net

I and my cats assess
the pickings of the day

Above us countless flakes
breathe in a holding shape

until slowly
they release their brakes

String Theory

My cats won't play with static toys:
they have to be balletic, with a puppeteer of human hands
to make a plain string dance.

The game becomes a battle, not of cat v string,
but of feline versus human
in multiple dimensions.

A flurry of movement, fur and claw,
is everything, a moment of release,
the creation of a wake

in which the instigator meets his shadow,
thrown in twisting, complex shapes,
outwitted by the light.

We all meet here, chasing our tails,
never quite seeing the point
but knowing how it moves, and will move on.

Zymurgy

Just north of Twice Brewed, Steel Rigg
looms over wet Northumberland -
the wall traces its ridge.

We trudge over peaks and troughs
            intense rain
slippery steps
            cattle caring less.

We reach a fort, its square footprint
a block between two hills,
look out through the mist,
imagine massing Picts,
our fortified retreat
a cold defence pitched in stone.

We've moved on
            clouds dividing
every few metres
            a split in time.

Our armour resists,
but still the rain gets in
and soon there is nothing to see
but a swirling fermentation
in which we stagger back,
our heads krausen.

Mousse - Mjódd - Meow

We talk in code
our references obscure, unique
inspired by song lyrics, games
or places that we visited together -
our language links us, a transparent thread
that strangers cannot touch.

The letters balance, pirouette
between our holding lips -
they've broken out from books and screens
and started inter-breeding
still only half-formed
and learning how to live.

We watch them do their tricks
applaud their wild weaving
and as they dance
we are entwined, our distant selves
connected by the patterns we create.

Outside is silence, or perhaps
it's so loud, we have filtered all else out
to cling to our tightrope of chattering -
we pull it taut, focus
try to think of a name for what we are.

Elephant in the Room

You loved elephants, or at least
that was the expectation:
it made last-minute presents easier.

But you only rated small ones -
babies, or the tiny silver pendants that you barely see
until you get up close - the elephants that hide in plain sight
and are never mentioned.

Now when I see your family,
you have become the elephant:
the silent link in the chain that once connected us:
so many of us, trunk to tail.

Nothing is said -
I fill the gap with memory,
a landscape that extends beyond the room,
imagining you out there,
a tiny elephant in all that space,
in search of those invisible words
we cannot find.

Drained

The drain was blocked.
It smells like death, you said,
like a putrid cadaver,
like the inside of hell.

I knelt, my gloved arm deep in the dark liquid,
tried to poke the unseen wedge with an old chopstick,
but nothing came loose - I fist-pumped
waves of soda crystals, swirling sludge...
They had one job: explode and scour. They drowned.

In the café, you told me again
how I had too many possessions,
how every time you came to visit
your heart sank
and how my home was insurmountable:
Why couldn't I let go?

Packages surround me; some Christmas gifts,
bags and boxes of dusty memories,
out-of-date cleaning materials, a dozen elephants,
muddy shoes and trousers that don't fit,
a bin liner of hats.

Later, I cracked open a Doom Bar, drained it.
The professionals have special rods, you said.
They go deep, they fix things.

Massage

We are acidic on the outside
the skin's mantle a barrier
secreted by sebaceous glands:
pH 4.5 to 6.2

Inside we're alkaline:
a milky mulch of organs and emotions
gloopy sentiment
packaged in functionality

I approach your rough exterior
with trepidation
your scars that tell a tale:
rash decisions
harsh consequences

But you do not like a soft touch
prefer a vigorous hand
manipulating fingers
that press and punish
with unrelenting questions

I leave reluctant prints
that leak but will not stain
and when my muscles tire
I withdraw
neutralised

Deli

This place isn't what it was:
the chairs displaced
the waiting staff
unfamiliar

They do have quiche
proper meats
helpings of salad
giant meringues
forager selection jam

They have music now
you wouldn't like
and the menu doesn't fold
the way it used to

The bathroom cubicle
a blanched Tardis
is still the same

After the breakfast bill
I wait a beat too long
for you to emerge

Modern Dance

A £1 purchase in a vinyl store, taken home,
reveals an inner sleeve, adorned
with felt-tip markings: a loving catalogue
of bands and band members, spelled out,
labelled with hearts and doodles, from the pen
of some unnamed teenage girl, in 1981.

This paper cover is a slice of history, recorded
louder and with greater clarity than each vibrating groove.
The needle skips past unknown landscapes
as I'm taken back to her, hearing her dream life played
through tinny speakers in an Ipswich flat,
her synthesised escape, rotating at 33rpm.

She travels, from a Berlin nightclub to Japan,
the crackle of dust her only barrier
between a life of glamour and her own, half-formed,
direction-fearing grasping in the dark,
the world so strange and empty. These sounds
are whispering only to her, and me.

She writes, and documents the names
in multi-coloured script, making her mark
and hiding it, a time capsule I'll find
all these years later. By now I guess she's lost
within the whirl of modern life, with teenagers herself,
deep in their MP3s, dancing in the data stream

and looking there for inspiration and connection -
on it goes, revolving. But if we scratch the surface
we can bind our time with echoes, then and now,
try to reach a region hidden and uncharted
that can bring us here together, as we journey
through the notes that make us who we are.

Reviews

1: 2010

The Spinning Top,
the latest effort by this
fair-to-middling playwright,
lacks finesse. In places it is heavy-
handed, and all-too-often it descends
into a quagmire of farce. It revolves
around a man who doesn't seem to know
his own mind - no, he flits from scene
to scene like a surrealist painting -
a telephone becomes
a chair?
and a coffee pot revolves
around a giant clock that strikes
irregularly, sometimes curtailing
a quite promising new story, and sending it in
some oblique direction. The audience is left
high up on a sheer cliff, peering down
at what remains of language
plot and sense.
The actors shift from character to character
and seem to improvise
when sticking to the script
would help us get a grip on things -
a firmer hand is what this needs.
Nobody says exactly what they mean
as if their enigmatic looks
are deeper than the words they speak.
The scenery's chaotic
all the walls are black
and on this canvas
we are meant to paint
our own conclusions.
Frankly, it's a mess.
Avoid. Two stars.

2: 2019

In the sequel, our young writer friend
has focused more on narrative:
things happen for a reason, there are consequences
and the plot is linear. There is less confusion.

It begins with a death. This is not what we expect.
The first act is a slow and steady meditation.
In the background gloom, other events occur,
but he ignores them, stares at us, soliloquises.

He steps to the piano, tries to play,
screams at no one in particular,
then he photographs the audience,
analyses our faces.

Players emerge from the stage piece by piece,
attempt to engage him with alternative scenarios,
intricate games, none of them real.
Eventually he laughs.

He walks, he travels.
He discovers people, places,
learns how to relax again,
the whole stage lit by one gigantic spotlight.

He finds pleasure seeing things
how they actually are, not how they seem to be.
Look at this piece of fruit, he says. *Isn't it wonderful?*
The other actors smirk behind their hands.

I won't spoil the ending, but I will say it plays out
in ways that none of us imagined.

Watch out for this one. Three and a half stars.